# ADVE MEMORIES

## JOURNAL & LOG BOOK

THIS BOOK BELONGS TO

_____
_____
_____

If you like this Adventures Memories Journal & Log Book, please leave a review.

Thank You -)

**My Easier Life**

# Table of Contents

| No | Travel location/Place name | Date | Rating | Page No |
|---|---|---|---|---|
| 1 | | | | 1-2 |
| 2 | | | | 3-4 |
| 3 | | | | 5-6 |
| 4 | | | | 7-8 |
| 5 | | | | 9-10 |
| 6 | | | | 11-12 |
| 7 | | | | 13-14 |
| 8 | | | | 15-16 |
| 9 | | | | 17-18 |
| 10 | | | | 19-20 |
| 11 | | | | 21-22 |
| 12 | | | | 23-24 |
| 13 | | | | 25-26 |
| 14 | | | | 27-28 |
| 15 | | | | 29-30 |
| 16 | | | | 31-32 |
| 17 | | | | 33-34 |
| 18 | | | | 35-36 |
| 19 | | | | 37-38 |
| 20 | | | | 39-40 |
| 21 | | | | 41-42 |
| 22 | | | | 43-44 |
| 23 | | | | 45-46 |
| 24 | | | | 47-48 |
| 25 | | | | 49-50 |

## Table Of Contents

| No | Travel location/Place name | Date | Rating | Page No |
|---|---|---|---|---|
| 26 | | | | 51-52 |
| 27 | | | | 53-54<br>55-56 |
| 28 | | | | 57-58 |
| 29 | | | | 59-60 |
| 30 | | | | 61-62 |
| 31 | | | | 63-64 |
| 32 | | | | 65-66 |
| 33 | | | | 67-68 |
| 34 | | | | 69-70 |
| 35 | | | | 71-72 |
| 36 | | | | 73-74 |
| 37 | | | | 75-76 |
| 38 | | | | 77-78 |
| 39 | | | | 79-80 |
| 40 | | | | 81-82 |
| 41 | | | | 83-84 |
| 42 | | | | 85-86 |
| 43 | | | | 87-88 |
| 44 | | | | 89-90 |
| 45 | | | | 91-92 |
| 46 | | | | 93-94 |
| 47 | | | | 95-96 |
| 48 | | | | 97-98 |
| 49 | | | | 99-100 |
| 50 | | | | 101-102 |

## Table Of Contents

| No | Travel location/Place name | Date | Rating | Page No |
|---|---|---|---|---|
| 51 | | | | 103-104 |
| 52 | | | | 105-106 |
| 53 | | | | 107-108 |
| 54 | | | | 109-110 |
| 55 | | | | 111-112 |
| 56 | | | | 113-114 |
| 57 | | | | 115-116 |
| 58 | | | | 117-118 |
| 59 | | | | 119-120 |
| 60 | | | | |
| | | | | |
| | | | | |
| | | | | |
| | | | | |
| | | | | |
| | | | | |
| | | | | |
| | | | | |
| | | | | |
| | | | | |
| | | | | |
| | | | | |
| | | | | |

| Travel Place Name : | | 01 |
|---|---|---|
| Rating : 1 2 3 4 5 6 7 8 9 10 | Date: | |

Location in the morning :
Location in the evening :
Travel time :          Distance :            Total cost :
Accommodation:              Address:
Website :                @:              IG:
Route (description):

Weather :    ☀    ⛅    ☁    ☁    🌧        Temperature :

Places visited/activities:

Contacts/New friends (name, e-mail, address, phone) :

One thing we'll always remember about this travel was :

If we visited here again we would be sure to :

Please to remember for the next-time (restaurants, places, attractions, etc) :

Favorite memories : 02

Notes :

Insert Photo Here

**Travel Place Name :**                                                                 03

Rating : 1 2 3 4 5 6 7 8 9 10          Date:

Location in the morning :
Location in the evening :
Travel time :             Distance :             Total cost :
Accommodation:                      Address:
Website :                      @:                      IG:
Route (description):

Weather :   ☀   ⛅   🌤   ☁   🌧            Temperature :

Places visited/activities:




Contacts/New friends (name, e-mail, address, phone) :



One thing we'll always remember about this travel was :



If we visited here again we would be sure to :



Please to remember for the next-time (restaurants, places, attractions, etc) :

Favorite memories : | 04 |

Notes :

Insert Photo Here

**Travel Place Name :**             05

**Rating :** 1 2 3 4 5 6 7 8 9 10     **Date:**

Location in the morning : ................................................................
Location in the evening : ................................................................
Travel time : .................    Distance : .................    Total cost : .................
Accommodation: ...........................    Address: ...........................
Website : ...........................    @: ...........................    IG: ...........................
Route (description): ................................................................
................................................................

Weather :    ☀    ⛅    🌤    🌧    ☁      Temperature : ...................

Places visited/activities:

................................................................
................................................................
................................................................
................................................................
................................................................

Contacts/New friends (name, e-mail, address, phone) :

................................................................
................................................................

One thing we'll always remember about this travel was :

................................................................
................................................................

If we visited here again we would be sure to :

................................................................
................................................................

Please to remember for the next-time (restaurants, places, attractions, etc) :

................................................................
................................................................
................................................................
................................................................
................................................................
................................................................

Favorite memories : 06

Notes :

Insert Photo Here

**Travel Place Name :**

07

Rating : 1 2 3 4 5 6 7 8 9 10          Date:

Location in the morning :
Location in the evening :
Travel time :           Distance :           Total cost :
Accommodation:          Address:
Website :          @:          IG:
Route (description):

Weather :   ☀   ⛅   🌤   ☁   🌧          Temperature :

Places visited/activities:

Contacts/New friends (name, e-mail, address, phone) :

One thing we'll always remember about this travel was :

If we visited here again we would be sure to :

Please to remember for the next-time (restaurants, places, attractions, etc) :

Favorite memories :

08

Notes :

Insert Photo Here

**Travel Place Name :**

09

Rating : 1 2 3 4 5 6 7 8 9 10     Date:

Location in the morning :
Location in the evening :
Travel time :          Distance :          Total cost :
Accommodation:              Address:
Website :              @:              IG:
Route (description):

Weather :   ☀   ⛅   🌤   ☁   🌧     Temperature :

Places visited/activities:




Contacts/New friends (name, e-mail, address, phone) :



One thing we'll always remember about this travel was :



If we visited here again we would be sure to :



Please to remember for the next-time (restaurants, places, attractions, etc) :

Favorite memories : | 10 |

Notes :

Insert Photo Here

| Travel Place Name : | | 11 |
|---|---|---|
| Rating : 1 2 3 4 5 6 7 8 9 10 | Date: | |

Location in the morning : ...........................................................................................................
Location in the evening : ...........................................................................................................

Travel time : ................... Distance : ................... Total cost : ...................
Accommodation: ........................... Address: ...........................................
Website : ........................... @: ........................... IG: ...........................
Route (description): ..............................................................................................

Weather :  ☀  ⛅  🌤  🌧  ⛈    Temperature : ...................

Places visited/activities:

..........................................................................................................
..........................................................................................................
..........................................................................................................
..........................................................................................................
..........................................................................................................

Contacts/New friends (name, e-mail, address, phone) :

..........................................................................................................
..........................................................................................................

One thing we'll always remember about this travel was :

..........................................................................................................
..........................................................................................................

If we visited here again we would be sure to :

..........................................................................................................
..........................................................................................................

Please to remember for the next-time (restaurants, places, attractions, etc) :

..........................................................................................................
..........................................................................................................
..........................................................................................................
..........................................................................................................
..........................................................................................................

Favorite memories :  12

----

Notes :

----

Insert Photo Here

| | **Travel Place Name :** | | 13 |
|---|---|---|---|
| | Rating : 1 2 3 4 5 6 7 8 9 10 | Date: | |

Location in the morning : _____
Location in the evening : _____
Travel time : _____  Distance : _____  Total cost : _____
Accommodation: _____  Address: _____
Website : _____  @: _____  IG: _____
Route (description): _____

Weather :  ☀  ⛅  🌤  🌧  🌦     Temperature : _____

Places visited/activities:

_____
_____
_____
_____
_____

Contacts/New friends (name, e-mail, address, phone) :

_____
_____

One thing we'll always remember about this travel was :

_____
_____

If we visited here again we would be sure to :

_____
_____

Please to remember for the next-time (restaurants, places, attractions, etc) :

_____
_____
_____
_____
_____

Favorite memories :   14

Notes :

Insert Photo Here

**Travel Place Name :**

Rating : 1 2 3 4 5 6 7 8 9 10      Date:

15

Location in the morning :
Location in the evening :
Travel time :          Distance :          Total cost :
Accommodation:          Address:
Website :          @:          IG:
Route (description):

Weather :   ☀   ⛅   🌤   ☁   🌧      Temperature :

Places visited/activities:




Contacts/New friends (name, e-mail, address, phone) :



One thing we'll always remember about this travel was :



If we visited here again we would be sure to :



Please to remember for the next-time (restaurants, places, attractions, etc) :

Favorite memories :

Notes :

Insert Photo Here

16

**Travel Place Name :**  17

Rating : 1 2 3 4 5 6 7 8 9 10  Date :

Location in the morning : ............................................................................................
Location in the evening : ............................................................................................
Travel time : ..................  Distance : ..................  Total cost : ..................
Accommodation: ..........................  Address: ..........................
Website : ..........................  @: ..........................  IG: ..........................
Route (description): ............................................................................................
............................................................................................

Weather :  ☀  ⛅  🌤  🌧  ⛈   Temperature : ..................

Places visited/activities:
............................................................................................
............................................................................................
............................................................................................
............................................................................................

Contacts/New friends (name, e-mail, address, phone) :
............................................................................................
............................................................................................

One thing we'll always remember about this travel was :
............................................................................................
............................................................................................

If we visited here again we would be sure to :
............................................................................................
............................................................................................

Please to remember for the next-time (restaurants, places, attractions, etc) :
............................................................................................
............................................................................................
............................................................................................
............................................................................................
............................................................................................

Favorite memories :

18

Notes :

Insert Photo Here

**Travel Place Name :**                                                    19

Rating : 1 2 3 4 5 6 7 8 9 10        Date:

Location in the morning :
Location in the evening :
Travel time :            Distance :            Total cost :
Accommodation:                  Address:
Website :               @:                IG:
Route (description):

Weather :   ☀  ⛅  🌦  ☁  🌧        Temperature :

Places visited/activities:

Contacts/New friends (name, e-mail, address, phone) :

One thing we'll always remember about this travel was :

If we visited here again we would be sure to :

Please to remember for the next-time (restaurants, places, attractions, etc) :

Favorite memories : 20

Notes :

Insert Photo Here

| | Travel Place Name : | | 21 |
|---|---|---|---|
| | Rating : 1 2 3 4 5 6 7 8 9 10 | Date: | |

Location in the morning : ........................................................................
Location in the evening : ........................................................................
Travel time : ................    Distance : ....................    Total cost : ................
Accommodation: .............................    Address: ........................................
Website : ........................................    @: ........................    IG: ................
Route (description): ........................................................................

Weather :   ☀   ⛅   🌤   ☁   🌧     Temperature : ................

Places visited/activities:

........................................................................
........................................................................
........................................................................
........................................................................
........................................................................
........................................................................

Contacts/New friends (name, e-mail, address, phone) :

........................................................................
........................................................................

One thing we'll always remember about this travel was :

........................................................................
........................................................................

If we visited here again we would be sure to :

........................................................................
........................................................................

Please to remember for the next-time (restaurants, places, attractions, etc) :

........................................................................
........................................................................
........................................................................
........................................................................
........................................................................

Favorite memories :

22

Notes :

Insert Photo Here

| Travel Place Name : | | 23 |
|---|---|---|
| Rating : 1 2 3 4 5 6 7 8 9 10 | Date: | |

Location in the morning : 
Location in the evening : 
Travel time :     Distance :     Total cost : 
Accommodation:     Address: 
Website :     @:     IG: 
Route (description): 

Weather :    ☀   ⛅   🌤   🌧   ☁     Temperature : 

Places visited/activities:




Contacts/New friends (name, e-mail, address, phone) :


One thing we'll always remember about this travel was :


If we visited here again we would be sure to :


Please to remember for the next-time (restaurants, places, attractions, etc) :

Favorite memories :

24

Notes :

Insert Photo Here

**Travel Place Name :**                                             25

Rating : 1 2 3 4 5 6 7 8 9 10        Date:

Location in the morning :
Location in the evening :
Travel time :          Distance :          Total cost :
Accommodation:              Address:
Website :              @:              IG:
Route (description):

Weather :   ☀  ⛅  🌤  ☁  🌧        Temperature :

Places visited/activities:




Contacts/New friends (name, e-mail, address, phone) :



One thing we'll always remember about this travel was :



If we visited here again we would be sure to :



Please to remember for the next-time (restaurants, places, attractions, etc) :

Favorite memories :

Notes :

Insert Photo Here

26

**Travel Place Name :** 27

Rating : 1 2 3 4 5 6 7 8 9 10   Date:

Location in the morning :
Location in the evening :
Travel time :          Distance :          Total cost :
Accommodation:          Address:
Website :          @:          IG:
Route (description):

Weather :   ☀   ⛅   ⛅   ☁   🌧      Temperature :

Places visited/activities:

Contacts/New friends (name, e-mail, address, phone) :

One thing we'll always remember about this travel was :

If we visited here again we would be sure to :

Please to remember for the next-time (restaurants, places, attractions, etc) :

Favorite memories :

Notes :

Insert Photo Here

| Travel Place Name : | | 29 |
|---|---|---|
| Rating : 1 2 3 4 5 6 7 8 9 10 | Date: | |

Location in the morning : ..................................................
Location in the evening : ..................................................
Travel time : ............ Distance : ............ Total cost : ............
Accommodation: ............ Address: ............
Website : ............ @: ............ IG: ............
Route (description): ..................................................

Weather : ☀ ⛅ 🌤 🌧 🌧 Temperature : ............

Places visited/activities:

..................................................
..................................................
..................................................
..................................................
..................................................

Contacts/New friends (name, e-mail, address, phone) :

..................................................
..................................................

One thing we'll always remember about this travel was :

..................................................
..................................................

If we visited here again we would be sure to :

..................................................
..................................................

Please to remember for the next-time (restaurants, places, attractions, etc) :

..................................................
..................................................
..................................................
..................................................
..................................................

Favorite memories : 30

Notes :

Insert Photo Here

| | **Travel Place Name :** | | 31 |
|---|---|---|---|
| | Rating : 1 2 3 4 5 6 7 8 9 10 | Date: | |

Location in the morning : ................................................................................
Location in the evening : ................................................................................
Travel time : ....................  Distance : ....................  Total cost : ....................
Accommodation: ............................  Address: ................................................
Website : ............................  @: ............................  IG: ............................
Route (description): ........................................................................................

Weather :   ☀   ⛅   🌤   ☁   🌧   Temperature : ....................

Places visited/activities:
........................................................................................
........................................................................................
........................................................................................
........................................................................................
........................................................................................

Contacts/New friends (name, e-mail, address, phone) :
........................................................................................
........................................................................................

One thing we'll always remember about this travel was :
........................................................................................
........................................................................................

If we visited here again we would be sure to :
........................................................................................
........................................................................................

Please to remember for the next-time (restaurants, places, attractions, etc) :
........................................................................................
........................................................................................
........................................................................................
........................................................................................
........................................................................................

Favorite memories :

Notes :

Insert Photo Here

| Travel Place Name : | | 33 |
|---|---|---|
| Rating : 1 2 3 4 5 6 7 8 9 10 | Date: | |

Location in the morning :
Location in the evening :
Travel time :          Distance :          Total cost :
Accommodation:                Address:
Website :          @:          IG:
Route (description):

Weather :   ☀   ⛅   ☁   🌧   🌦          Temperature :

Places visited/activities:




Contacts/New friends (name, e-mail, address, phone) :



One thing we'll always remember about this travel was :



If we visited here again we would be sure to :



Please to remember for the next-time (restaurants, places, attractions, etc) :

Favorite memories :  34

Notes :

Insert Photo Here

| Travel Place Name : | | 35 |
|---|---|---|
| Rating : 1 2 3 4 5 6 7 8 9 10 | Date: | |

Location in the morning :
Location in the evening :
Travel time :          Distance :          Total cost :
Accommodation:          Address:
Website :          @:          IG:
Route (description):

Weather :   ☀   ⛅   🌤   ☁   🌧          Temperature :
Places visited/activities:

Contacts/New friends (name, e-mail, address, phone) :

One thing we'll always remember about this travel was :

If we visited here again we would be sure to :

Please to remember for the next-time (restaurants, places, attractions, etc) :

Favorite memories :

36

Notes :

Insert Photo Here

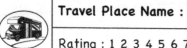

**Travel Place Name :**

Rating : 1 2 3 4 5 6 7 8 9 10     Date:

Location in the morning :
Location in the evening :
Travel time :          Distance :          Total cost :
Accommodation:          Address:
Website :          @:          IG:
Route (description):

Weather :          Temperature :

Places visited/activities:




Contacts/New friends (name, e-mail, address, phone) :



One thing we'll always remember about this travel was :



If we visited here again we would be sure to :



Please to remember for the next-time (restaurants, places, attractions, etc) :

Favorite memories : 38

Notes :

Insert Photo Here

**Travel Place Name :** 39

**Rating :** 1 2 3 4 5 6 7 8 9 10     **Date:**

Location in the morning :
Location in the evening :
Travel time :          Distance :            Total cost :
Accommodation:              Address:
Website :              @:              IG:
Route (description):

Weather :   ☀   ⛅   ⛅   ☁   🌧          Temperature :

Places visited/activities:

Contacts/New friends (name, e-mail, address, phone) :

One thing we'll always remember about this travel was :

If we visited here again we would be sure to :

Please to remember for the next-time (restaurants, places, attractions, etc) :

Favorite memories :                                                                 | 40 |

Notes :

Insert Photo Here

**Travel Place Name :**

Rating : 1 2 3 4 5 6 7 8 9 10

Date :

41

Location in the morning :
Location in the evening :
Travel time :          Distance :          Total cost :
Accommodation :          Address :
Website :          @ :          IG :
Route (description) :

Weather :  ☀  ⛅  🌤  🌧  ☁          Temperature :

Places visited/activities :

Contacts/New friends (name, e-mail, address, phone) :

One thing we'll always remember about this travel was :

If we visited here again we would be sure to :

Please to remember for the next-time (restaurants, places, attractions, etc) :

Favorite memories :

42

Notes :

Insert Photo Here

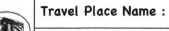 **Travel Place Name :** | 43
--- | ---
Rating : 1 2 3 4 5 6 7 8 9 10 | Date:

Location in the morning :
Location in the evening :
Travel time :     Distance :     Total cost :
Accommodation:     Address:
Website :     @:     IG:
Route (description):

Weather :  ☀  🌤  ⛅  ☁  🌧      Temperature :

Places visited/activities:




Contacts/New friends (name, e-mail, address, phone) :



One thing we'll always remember about this travel was :



If we visited here again we would be sure to :



Please to remember for the next-time (restaurants, places, attractions, etc) :

Favorite memories :  | 44 |

Notes :

Insert Photo Here

**Travel Place Name :**                    45

Rating : 1 2 3 4 5 6 7 8 9 10     Date:

Location in the morning :
Location in the evening :
Travel time :      Distance :      Total cost :
Accommodation:      Address:
Website :      @:      IG:
Route (description):

Weather :    ☀   ⛅   🌥   ☁   🌧      Temperature :

Places visited/activities:




Contacts/New friends (name, e-mail, address, phone) :



One thing we'll always remember about this travel was :



If we visited here again we would be sure to :



Please to remember for the next-time (restaurants, places, attractions, etc) :

Favorite memories : 46

Notes :

Insert Photo Here

**Travel Place Name :**

Rating : 1 2 3 4 5 6 7 8 9 10

Date:

47

Location in the morning :
Location in the evening :
Travel time :          Distance :          Total cost :
Accommodation:          Address:
Website :          @:          IG:
Route (description):

Weather :   ☀   ⛅   🌤   🌧   ⛈          Temperature :

Places visited/activities:




Contacts/New friends (name, e-mail, address, phone) :


One thing we'll always remember about this travel was :


If we visited here again we would be sure to :


Please to remember for the next-time (restaurants, places, attractions, etc) :

Favorite memories :

48

Notes :

Insert Photo Here

| 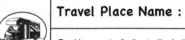 | **Travel Place Name :** | | 49 |
|---|---|---|---|
| | Rating : 1 2 3 4 5 6 7 8 9 10 | Date: | |

Location in the morning : ............................................................................................................
Location in the evening : ............................................................................................................
Travel time : ................         Distance : ......................         Total cost : ...........................
Accommodation: ..............................         Address: ..................................................
Website : ............................................         @: ...............................         IG: ..............
Route (description): ....................................................................................................
..................................................................................................................................

Weather :   ☀   ⛅   🌤   ☁   🌧         Temperature : ...........................

Places visited/activities:

..................................................................................................................................
..................................................................................................................................
..................................................................................................................................
..................................................................................................................................
..................................................................................................................................

Contacts/New friends (name, e-mail, address, phone) :

..................................................................................................................................
..................................................................................................................................

One thing we'll always remember about this travel was :

..................................................................................................................................
..................................................................................................................................

If we visited here again we would be sure to :

..................................................................................................................................
..................................................................................................................................

Please to remember for the next-time (restaurants, places, attractions, etc) :

..................................................................................................................................
..................................................................................................................................
..................................................................................................................................
..................................................................................................................................
..................................................................................................................................

Favorite memories : | 50 |

Notes :

---

Insert Photo Here

**Travel Place Name :** 51

Rating : 1 2 3 4 5 6 7 8 9 10    Date:

Location in the morning : ........................................................................................................
Location in the evening : ........................................................................................................
Travel time : ................    Distance : ................    Total cost : ................
Accommodation: ........................    Address: ........................
Website : ........................    @: ........................    IG: ........................
Route (description): ........................................................................................................

Weather :   ☀   ⛅   🌤   ☁   🌧      Temperature : ................

Places visited/activities:

........................................................................................................
........................................................................................................
........................................................................................................
........................................................................................................
........................................................................................................
........................................................................................................

Contacts/New friends (name, e-mail, address, phone) :

........................................................................................................
........................................................................................................
........................................................................................................

One thing we'll always remember about this travel was :

........................................................................................................
........................................................................................................
........................................................................................................

If we visited here again we would be sure to :

........................................................................................................
........................................................................................................
........................................................................................................

Please to remember for the next-time (restaurants, places, attractions, etc) :

........................................................................................................
........................................................................................................
........................................................................................................
........................................................................................................
........................................................................................................
........................................................................................................

Favorite memories : 52

Notes :

Insert Photo Here

**Travel Place Name :**     53

Rating : 1 2 3 4 5 6 7 8 9 10    Date:

Location in the morning :
Location in the evening :
Travel time :     Distance :     Total cost :
Accommodation:     Address:
Website :     @:     IG:
Route (description):

Weather :    ☀   ⛅   🌤   🌧   ☁     Temperature :

Places visited/activities:




Contacts/New friends (name, e-mail, address, phone) :


One thing we'll always remember about this travel was :


If we visited here again we would be sure to :


Please to remember for the next-time (restaurants, places, attractions, etc) :

Favorite memories : 54

Notes :

Insert Photo Here

**Travel Place Name :**

Rating : 1 2 3 4 5 6 7 8 9 10     Date:

55

Location in the morning :
Location in the evening :
Travel time :          Distance :          Total cost :
Accommodation:               Address:
Website :           @:           IG:
Route (description):

Weather :   ☀   ⛅   🌤   ☁   🌧         Temperature :

Places visited/activities:



Contacts/New friends (name, e-mail, address, phone) :



One thing we'll always remember about this travel was :



If we visited here again we would be sure to :



Please to remember for the next-time (restaurants, places, attractions, etc) :

Favorite memories :

Notes :

Insert Photo Here

**Travel Place Name :** 57

Rating : 1 2 3 4 5 6 7 8 9 10         Date:

Location in the morning :
Location in the evening :
Travel time :          Distance :          Total cost :
Accommodation:               Address:
Website :               @:               IG:
Route (description):

Weather :   ☀   ⛅   🌦   ☁   🌧         Temperature :

Places visited/activities:




Contacts/New friends (name, e-mail, address, phone) :



One thing we'll always remember about this travel was :



If we visited here again we would be sure to :



Please to remember for the next-time (restaurants, places, attractions, etc) :

Favorite memories :

Notes :

Insert Photo Here

**Travel Place Name :**

Rating : 1 2 3 4 5 6 7 8 9 10     Date :

Location in the morning :
Location in the evening :
Travel time :          Distance :          Total cost :
Accommodation :          Address :
Website :          @ :          IG :
Route (description) :

Weather :   ☀   ⛅   🌤   ☁   🌧          Temperature :

Places visited/activities :




Contacts/New friends (name, e-mail, address, phone) :


One thing we'll always remember about this travel was :


If we visited here again we would be sure to :


Please to remember for the next-time (restaurants, places, attractions, etc) :

Favorite memories : 60

Notes :

Insert Photo Here

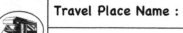

**Travel Place Name :**

Rating : 1 2 3 4 5 6 7 8 9 10         Date:

Location in the morning :
Location in the evening :
Travel time :          Distance :          Total cost :
Accommodation:              Address:
Website :              @:              IG:
Route (description):

Weather :   ☀   ⛅   ⛅   ☁   🌧          Temperature :

Places visited/activities:




Contacts/New friends (name, e-mail, address, phone) :



One thing we'll always remember about this travel was :



If we visited here again we would be sure to :



Please to remember for the next-time (restaurants, places, attractions, etc) :

Favorite memories :

Notes :

```
Insert Photo Here
```

**Travel Place Name :**                                                                 63

Rating : 1 2 3 4 5 6 7 8 9 10      Date:

Location in the morning :
Location in the evening :
Travel time :           Distance :           Total cost :
Accommodation:                    Address:
Website :              @:              IG:
Route (description):

Weather :   ☼   ⛅   🌤   ☁   🌧        Temperature :

Places visited/activities:




Contacts/New friends (name, e-mail, address, phone) :



One thing we'll always remember about this travel was :



If we visited here again we would be sure to :



Please to remember for the next-time (restaurants, places, attractions, etc) :

Favorite memories :

64

Notes :

Insert Photo Here

**Travel Place Name :**

**Rating :** 1 2 3 4 5 6 7 8 9 10

**Date:**

65

Location in the morning :
Location in the evening :
Travel time :          Distance :          Total cost :
Accommodation:          Address:
Website :          @:          IG:
Route (description):

Weather :   ☀   ⛅   🌥   🌧   🌦          Temperature :

Places visited/activities:




Contacts/New friends (name, e-mail, address, phone) :


One thing we'll always remember about this travel was :


If we visited here again we would be sure to :


Please to remember for the next-time (restaurants, places, attractions, etc) :

Favorite memories :

66

Notes :

Insert Photo Here

**Travel Place Name :**

Rating : 1 2 3 4 5 6 7 8 9 10    Date:

Location in the morning :
Location in the evening :
Travel time :          Distance :          Total cost :
Accommodation:          Address:
Website :          @:          IG:
Route (description):

Weather :    ☀  ⛅  🌤  ☁  🌧          Temperature :

Places visited/activities:

Contacts/New friends (name, e-mail, address, phone) :

One thing we'll always remember about this travel was :

If we visited here again we would be sure to :

Please to remember for the next-time (restaurants, places, attractions, etc) :

Favorite memories :

Notes :

Insert Photo Here

| Travel Place Name : | | 69 |
|---|---|---|
| Rating : 1 2 3 4 5 6 7 8 9 10 | Date: | |

Location in the morning : _____
Location in the evening : _____
Travel time : _____  Distance : _____  Total cost : _____
Accommodation: _____  Address: _____
Website : _____  @: _____  IG: _____
Route (description): _____

Weather :   ☀   ⛅   🌤   ☁   🌧   Temperature : _____

Places visited/activities:
_____
_____
_____
_____
_____

Contacts/New friends (name, e-mail, address, phone) :
_____
_____

One thing we'll always remember about this travel was :
_____
_____

If we visited here again we would be sure to :
_____
_____

Please to remember for the next-time (restaurants, places, attractions, etc) :
_____
_____
_____
_____
_____

Favorite memories :

70

Notes :

Insert Photo Here

| Travel Place Name : | 71 |
|---|---|
| Rating : 1 2 3 4 5 6 7 8 9 10 | Date: |

Location in the morning :
Location in the evening :
Travel time :        Distance :            Total cost :
Accommodation:                Address:
Website :                @:             IG:
Route (description):

Weather :   ☀  ⛅  🌤  🌧  ⛈        Temperature :

Places visited/activities:




Contacts/New friends (name, e-mail, address, phone) :



One thing we'll always remember about this travel was :



If we visited here again we would be sure to :



Please to remember for the next-time (restaurants, places, attractions, etc) :

Favorite memories : 72

Notes :

Insert Photo Here

| | **Travel Place Name :** | | 73 |
|---|---|---|---|
| | Rating : 1 2 3 4 5 6 7 8 9 10 | Date: | |

Location in the morning :
Location in the evening :
Travel time :        Distance :        Total cost :
Accommodation:        Address:
Website :        @:        IG:
Route (description):

Weather :   ☀  ⛅  🌤  ☁  🌧        Temperature :

Places visited/activities:

Contacts/New friends (name, e-mail, address, phone) :

One thing we'll always remember about this travel was :

If we visited here again we would be sure to :

Please to remember for the next-time (restaurants, places, attractions, etc) :

Favorite memories :

74

Notes :

Insert Photo Here

| Travel Place Name : | | 75 |
|---|---|---|
| Rating : 1 2 3 4 5 6 7 8 9 10 | Date: | |

Location in the morning :
Location in the evening :
Travel time :      Distance :      Total cost :
Accommodation:      Address:
Website :      @:      IG:
Route (description):

Weather :      Temperature :

Places visited/activities:




Contacts/New friends (name, e-mail, address, phone) :


One thing we'll always remember about this travel was :


If we visited here again we would be sure to :


Please to remember for the next-time (restaurants, places, attractions, etc) :

Favorite memories :  76

Notes :

Insert Photo Here

| | **Travel Place Name :** | | 77 |
|---|---|---|---|
| | Rating : 1 2 3 4 5 6 7 8 9 10 | Date: | |

Location in the morning : _____
Location in the evening : _____
Travel time : _____   Distance : _____   Total cost : _____
Accommodation: _____   Address: _____
Website : _____   @: _____   IG: _____
Route (description): _____

Weather :   ☀  ⛅  🌤  ☁  🌧   Temperature : _____

Places visited/activities:

_____
_____
_____
_____
_____

Contacts/New friends (name, e-mail, address, phone) :

_____
_____

One thing we'll always remember about this travel was :

_____
_____

If we visited here again we would be sure to :

_____
_____

Please to remember for the next-time (restaurants, places, attractions, etc) :

_____
_____
_____
_____
_____

Favorite memories :  78

Notes :

Insert Photo Here

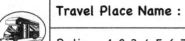

**Travel Place Name :**

Rating : 1 2 3 4 5 6 7 8 9 10      Date:

Location in the morning :
Location in the evening :
Travel time :          Distance :          Total cost :
Accommodation:              Address:
Website :              @:              IG:
Route (description):

Weather :   ☀   ⛅   🌤   ☁   🌧          Temperature :

Places visited/activities:




Contacts/New friends (name, e-mail, address, phone) :



One thing we'll always remember about this travel was :



If we visited here again we would be sure to :



Please to remember for the next-time (restaurants, places, attractions, etc) :

Favorite memories : 80

Notes :

Insert Photo Here

| **Travel Place Name :** | | 81 |
|---|---|---|
| Rating : 1 2 3 4 5 6 7 8 9 10 | Date : | |

Location in the morning : ........................................................................................................
Location in the evening : ........................................................................................................
Travel time : ................  Distance : ..................  Total cost : ..................
Accommodation: ............................  Address: ........................................
Website : ............................  @: ............................  IG: ............................
Route (description): ........................................................................................................

Weather :  ☀  ⛅  🌦  ☁  🌧     Temperature : ............................

Places visited/activities:

........................................................................................................
........................................................................................................
........................................................................................................
........................................................................................................

Contacts/New friends (name, e-mail, address, phone) :

........................................................................................................
........................................................................................................

One thing we'll always remember about this travel was :

........................................................................................................
........................................................................................................

If we visited here again we would be sure to :

........................................................................................................
........................................................................................................

Please to remember for the next-time (restaurants, places, attractions, etc) :

........................................................................................................
........................................................................................................
........................................................................................................
........................................................................................................
........................................................................................................

Favorite memories :

| 82 |

Notes :

Insert Photo Here

**Travel Place Name :**             83

**Rating :** 1 2 3 4 5 6 7 8 9 10     **Date:**

Location in the morning :

Location in the evening :

Travel time :     Distance :     Total cost :

Accommodation:     Address:

Website :     @:     IG:

Route (description):

Weather : ☀ ⛅ 🌤 ☁ 🌧     Temperature :

Places visited/activities:

Contacts/New friends (name, e-mail, address, phone) :

One thing we'll always remember about this travel was :

If we visited here again we would be sure to :

Please to remember for the next-time (restaurants, places, attractions, etc) :

Favorite memories :

Notes :

Insert Photo Here

**Travel Place Name :**

Rating : 1 2 3 4 5 6 7 8 9 10        Date:

Location in the morning :
Location in the evening :
Travel time :          Distance :          Total cost :
Accommodation:                 Address:
Website :                 @:                 IG:
Route (description):

Weather :   ☀  ⛅  🌥  ☁  🌧        Temperature :

Places visited/activities:

Contacts/New friends (name, e-mail, address, phone) :

One thing we'll always remember about this travel was :

If we visited here again we would be sure to :

Please to remember for the next-time (restaurants, places, attractions, etc) :

Favorite memories :

Notes :

Insert Photo Here

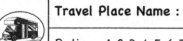

**Travel Place Name :**

Rating : 1 2 3 4 5 6 7 8 9 10        Date:

Location in the morning :
Location in the evening :
Travel time :              Distance :              Total cost :
Accommodation:                    Address:
Website :                    @:              IG:
Route (description):

Weather :   ☀  ⛅  🌤  ☁  🌧        Temperature :

Places visited/activities:




Contacts/New friends (name, e-mail, address, phone) :



One thing we'll always remember about this travel was :



If we visited here again we would be sure to :



Please to remember for the next-time (restaurants, places, attractions, etc) :

Favorite memories :

88

Notes :

Insert Photo Here

| | **Travel Place Name :** | | 89 |
|---|---|---|---|
| | Rating : 1 2 3 4 5 6 7 8 9 10 | Date: | |

Location in the morning : _____
Location in the evening : _____
Travel time : _____   Distance : _____   Total cost : _____
Accommodation: _____   Address: _____
Website : _____   @: _____   IG: _____
Route (description): _____

Weather :  ☀  ⛅  🌤  🌧  ⛈     Temperature : _____

Places visited/activities:
_____
_____
_____
_____
_____


Contacts/New friends (name, e-mail, address, phone) :
_____
_____

One thing we'll always remember about this travel was :
_____
_____

If we visited here again we would be sure to :
_____
_____

Please to remember for the next-time (restaurants, places, attractions, etc) :
_____
_____
_____
_____
_____
_____

Favorite memories : 90

Notes :

Insert Photo Here

**Travel Place Name :**

Rating : 1 2 3 4 5 6 7 8 9 10      Date:

Location in the morning : ................................................................
Location in the evening : ................................................................
Travel time : ..................    Distance : ..................    Total cost : ..................
Accommodation: ........................    Address: ........................
Website : ..................    @: ..................    IG: ..................
Route (description): ................................................................

Weather :   ☀   ⛅   🌤   ☁   🌧      Temperature : ..................

Places visited/activities:

........................................................................
........................................................................
........................................................................
........................................................................
........................................................................

Contacts/New friends (name, e-mail, address, phone) :

........................................................................
........................................................................

One thing we'll always remember about this travel was :

........................................................................
........................................................................

If we visited here again we would be sure to :

........................................................................
........................................................................

Please to remember for the next-time (restaurants, places, attractions, etc) :

........................................................................
........................................................................
........................................................................
........................................................................
........................................................................

Favorite memories :

Notes :

Insert Photo Here

**Travel Place Name :** 93

Rating : 1 2 3 4 5 6 7 8 9 10      Date:

Location in the morning :
Location in the evening :
Travel time :          Distance :          Total cost :
Accommodation:           Address:
Website :           @:           IG:
Route (description):

Weather :   ☀   ⛅   🌤   ☁   🌧      Temperature :

Places visited/activities:




Contacts/New friends (name, e-mail, address, phone) :


One thing we'll always remember about this travel was :


If we visited here again we would be sure to :


Please to remember for the next-time (restaurants, places, attractions, etc) :

Favorite memories :

Notes :

Insert Photo Here

| | **Travel Place Name :** | | 95 |
|---|---|---|---|
| | Rating : 1 2 3 4 5 6 7 8 9 10 | Date: | |

Location in the morning : ........................................................
Location in the evening : ........................................................

Travel time : ................  Distance : ................  Total cost : ................
Accommodation: ........................  Address: ........................
Website : ........................  @: ........................  IG: ........................
Route (description): ........................................................

Weather :   ☀   ⛅   🌤   🌧   🌦      Temperature : ................

Places visited/activities:

........................................................
........................................................
........................................................
........................................................
........................................................

Contacts/New friends (name, e-mail, address, phone) :

........................................................
........................................................

One thing we'll always remember about this travel was :

........................................................
........................................................

If we visited here again we would be sure to :

........................................................
........................................................

Please to remember for the next-time (restaurants, places, attractions, etc) :

........................................................
........................................................
........................................................
........................................................
........................................................
........................................................

Favorite memories :

| 96 |

Notes :

Insert Photo Here

**Travel Place Name :** 97

Rating : 1 2 3 4 5 6 7 8 9 10 | Date:

Location in the morning :
Location in the evening :
Travel time :     Distance :     Total cost :
Accommodation:     Address:
Website :     @:     IG:
Route (description):

Weather :      Temperature :

Places visited/activities:

Contacts/New friends (name, e-mail, address, phone) :

One thing we'll always remember about this travel was :

If we visited here again we would be sure to :

Please to remember for the next-time (restaurants, places, attractions, etc) :

Favorite memories :

Notes :

Insert Photo Here

**Travel Place Name :**

Rating : 1 2 3 4 5 6 7 8 9 10    Date:

Location in the morning :
Location in the evening :
Travel time :         Distance :          Total cost :
Accommodation:            Address:
Website :           @:            IG:
Route (description):

Weather :  ☀  ⛅  🌦  ☁  🌧     Temperature :

Places visited/activities:




Contacts/New friends (name, e-mail, address, phone) :



One thing we'll always remember about this travel was :



If we visited here again we would be sure to :



Please to remember for the next-time (restaurants, places, attractions, etc) :

Favorite memories : 100

Notes :

Insert Photo Here

**Travel Place Name :**     101

**Rating :** 1 2 3 4 5 6 7 8 9 10     **Date :**

Location in the morning :
Location in the evening :
Travel time :     Distance :     Total cost :
Accommodation :     Address :
Website :     @ :     IG :
Route (description) :

Weather : ☀ ⛅ 🌦 ☁ 🌧     Temperature :

Places visited/activities :




Contacts/New friends (name, e-mail, address, phone) :


One thing we'll always remember about this travel was :


If we visited here again we would be sure to :


Please to remember for the next-time (restaurants, places, attractions, etc) :

Favorite memories :

Notes :

Insert Photo Here

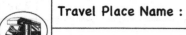

**Travel Place Name :**

Rating : 1 2 3 4 5 6 7 8 9 10     Date:

Location in the morning :
Location in the evening :
Travel time :          Distance :          Total cost :
Accommodation:              Address:
Website :          @:          IG:
Route (description):

Weather :    ☀    ⛅    🌤    ☁    🌧          Temperature :

Places visited/activities:




Contacts/New friends (name, e-mail, address, phone) :



One thing we'll always remember about this travel was :



If we visited here again we would be sure to :



Please to remember for the next-time (restaurants, places, attractions, etc) :

Favorite memories :

104

Notes :

Insert Photo Here

**Travel Place Name :** 105

Rating : 1 2 3 4 5 6 7 8 9 10     Date :

Location in the morning :
Location in the evening :
Travel time :          Distance :          Total cost :
Accommodation :          Address :
Website :          @ :          IG :
Route (description) :

Weather :   ☀   ⛅   🌤   ☁   🌧          Temperature :

Places visited/activities :

Contacts/New friends (name, e-mail, address, phone) :

One thing we'll always remember about this travel was :

If we visited here again we would be sure to :

Please to remember for the next-time (restaurants, places, attractions, etc) :

Favorite memories : | 106 |

Notes :

Insert Photo Here

| **Travel Place Name :** | | 107 |
|---|---|---|
| Rating : 1 2 3 4 5 6 7 8 9 10 | Date: | |

Location in the morning : ...................................................................................................
Location in the evening : ...................................................................................................

Travel time : ........................... Distance : ........................... Total cost : ...........................
Accommodation: ........................... Address: ...........................
Website : ........................... @: ........................... IG: ...........................
Route (description): ...........................

Weather :  ☀  ⛅  🌦  ☁  🌧   Temperature : ...........................

Places visited/activities:

...........................................................................................................................
...........................................................................................................................
...........................................................................................................................
...........................................................................................................................

Contacts/New friends (name, e-mail, address, phone) :

...........................................................................................................................
...........................................................................................................................

One thing we'll always remember about this travel was :

...........................................................................................................................
...........................................................................................................................

If we visited here again we would be sure to :

...........................................................................................................................
...........................................................................................................................

Please to remember for the next-time (restaurants, places, attractions, etc) :

...........................................................................................................................
...........................................................................................................................
...........................................................................................................................
...........................................................................................................................
...........................................................................................................................

Favorite memories :

108

Notes :

Insert Photo Here

**Travel Place Name :**

Rating : 1 2 3 4 5 6 7 8 9 10    Date:

Location in the morning :
Location in the evening :
Travel time :           Distance :           Total cost :
Accommodation:                   Address:
Website :                @:                IG:
Route (description):

Weather :   ☀   ⛅   🌤   ☁   🌧     Temperature :

Places visited/activities:




Contacts/New friends (name, e-mail, address, phone) :



One thing we'll always remember about this travel was :



If we visited here again we would be sure to :



Please to remember for the next-time (restaurants, places, attractions, etc) :

Favorite memories :

110

Notes :

---

Insert Photo Here

**Travel Place Name :**

Rating : 1 2 3 4 5 6 7 8 9 10     Date:

Location in the morning :
Location in the evening :
Travel time :          Distance :          Total cost :
Accommodation:          Address:
Website :          @:          IG:
Route (description):

Weather :     ☀  ⛅  🌦  ☁  🌧          Temperature :

Places visited/activities:




Contacts/New friends (name, e-mail, address, phone) :



One thing we'll always remember about this travel was :



If we visited here again we would be sure to :



Please to remember for the next-time (restaurants, places, attractions, etc) :

Favorite memories :

Notes :

Insert Photo Here

| Travel Place Name : | | 113 |
|---|---|---|
| Rating : 1 2 3 4 5 6 7 8 9 10 | Date: | |

Location in the morning : ............................................................................................
Location in the evening : ............................................................................................

Travel time : ..................... Distance : ..................... Total cost : .....................
Accommodation: ............................. Address: .............................................
Website : ............................. @: ............................. IG: .............................
Route (description): ............................................................................................

Weather :  ☀  ⛅  🌤  ☁  🌧     Temperature : .....................

Places visited/activities:

............................................................................................
............................................................................................
............................................................................................
............................................................................................
............................................................................................

Contacts/New friends (name, e-mail, address, phone) :

............................................................................................
............................................................................................

One thing we'll always remember about this travel was :

............................................................................................
............................................................................................

If we visited here again we would be sure to :

............................................................................................
............................................................................................

Please to remember for the next-time (restaurants, places, attractions, etc) :

............................................................................................
............................................................................................
............................................................................................
............................................................................................
............................................................................................
............................................................................................

Favorite memories :

Notes :

Insert Photo Here

Made in United States
Orlando, FL
01 March 2023

30579564R00068